Tales of the Elven Dewdrops

In the forest's soft embrace,
Where moonlight weaves its thread,
Elves dance beneath the stars,
With whispers left unsaid.

Each dewdrop holds a tale,
Of laughter, love, and grace,
Reflecting dreams of old,
In their gentle embrace.

Through shadows they take flight,
On wings of silver light,
Chasing bright fireflies,
In the heart of the night.

The brook hums a sweet song,
As time begins to bend,
A symphony of dusk,
That never seems to end.

Beneath the ancient trees,
Their secrets softly shared,
The elven dew drops fall,
In moments deeply cared.

Glistening Fruits of the Faerie Realm

In gardens lush and bright,
With colors rich and rare,
The fruits of faerie lore,
Hang heavily in the air.

Golden apples gleam and shine,
With sweet enchantments spun,
While berries burst like laughter,
Beneath the glowing sun.

From blossoms soft and rare,
The nectar flows like gold,
A sip can grant a wish,
A story yet untold.

In twilight's gentle glow,
They shimmer with delight,
Inviting all who wander,
To join their feast tonight.

Each flavor tells a tale,
Of magic, hope, and mirth,
The fruits of faerie dreams,
Bring joy upon the earth.

The Magic of Luminous Glades

In glades where shadows play,
And lanterns softly gleam,
The world transforms with night,
In a starry, silver dream.

Mossy paths lead us near,
To secrets buried deep,
Where moonbeams touch the ground,
And lost dreams often seep.

With every step we take,
The magic starts to swirl,
As fireflies weave light,
In a mystical twirl.

The whispers of the trees,
Compose a gentle tune,
A lullaby of hope,
Beneath the watchful moon.

In luminous glades we find,
A spark, a joyful bliss,
A dance of purest light,
In a faerie's tender kiss.

Enchanted Jewels of Nocturnal Hush

In the quiet of the night,
Where secrets softly gleam,
Enchanted jewels awaken,
In shadows where they dream.

The stars hang like crystals,
Adorned in velvet skies,
While moonlit gems reflect,
The wishes of our sighs.

Each jewel tells a story,
Of love, of loss, of cheer,
In whispers wrapped in starlight,
That only night can hear.

They sparkle with a promise,
Of magic yet to come,
In the stillness of the hour,
To the beating of a drum.

With every twinkling glance,
The world seems to renew,
In the enchanted hush of night,
Where dreams can come true.

Whispers of Mossy Globes

In forests deep, where shadows play,
The whispered tales of night and day.
Mossy globes, a velvet tour,
Nature's secrets, old and pure.

Beneath the boughs, the whispers weave,
A tapestry that none deceives.
Each soft breath, a story told,
Of ancient woods, of dreams of old.

With every step, a gentle sigh,
Where spirits dance and willows cry.
In glades adorned with emerald hue,
The mossy globes hold worlds anew.

Enchanted Spheres in Glistening Glades

In glistening glades where fairies gleam,
Enchanted spheres reflect the dream.
A palette bright of color swirl,
In every breeze, their magic twirl.

They hover close, with laughter sweet,
A dance of light, a playful feat.
Among the blooms, the orbs ignite,
A symphony of pure delight.

The sunlit beams through branches fall,
On floating spheres, a radiant call.
The heart of nature, pure and true,
In glades adorned, adventure's cue.

The Fairy's Grotto of Twisted Pearls

In caves where shadows softly play,
The fairy's grotto hides away.
Twisted pearls, a treasure bright,
Glimmering softly in the night.

A secret world, where whispers reign,
Bound by dreams and silken chain.
Each pearl a wish, a glowing light,
A promise held by moon's soft flight.

With every spark, the stories wake,
A dance of fate, a heart to break.
In twisted paths, the echoes swell,
Within the grotto, magic dwells.

Dew-Kissed Mysteries Beneath the Canopy

Beneath the canopy of green,
Lie mysteries that few have seen.
Dew-kissed webs, like jewels spun,
In morning light, they gleam and run.

A chorus sings of life anew,
In whispered notes that wander through.
With every leaf, a story grows,
Of hidden trails that nature knows.

The mist unfolds as daylight breaks,
Revealing paths the morning makes.
In the embrace of ancient trees,
Dew-kissed dreams float on the breeze.

Phosphorescent Dreamscapes of Enchantment

In twilight's grasp where whispers tread,
A carpet woven, dreams are bred.
The stars align in silver streams,
Awaking hearts, igniting dreams.

Through misty paths, the lanterns glow,
With secrets wrapped in twilight's flow.
Each corner holds a tale untold,
Of magic realms, both brave and bold.

The air is thick with sweet perfume,
As fairies dance in quiet rooms.
A cottage near the bubbling brook,
Holds stories deep in every nook.

Lost in a world where time stands still,
The moonlit frame, a gentle thrill.
Where every shadow hides a spark,
And daylight fades into the dark.

With every breath, enchantment swells,
In phosphorescent, whispered spells.
A dreamers' haven, bright and rare,
Where hope is found, suspended air.

Dappled Horizons Beyond the Glade

A break of dawn spills golden light,
Through canopies, a wondrous sight.
The forest sighs, a gentle song,
As life awakens, bold and strong.

Beneath the boughs of ancient trees,
The softest whispers reach the knees.
In dappled shade, the fairies play,
With laughter woven into day.

A brook nearby sings crystal clear,
As nature's choir draws ever near.
In harmony, the leaves do sway,
A dance of time that will not fray.

Beyond the glade, horizons call,
With colors rich, enchanting all.
Each step we take, a world anew,
In breezes soft, hearts will imbue.

Emerald meadows, wild and free,
Invite us forth, a jubilee.
Where dreams align with every breath,
In nature's arms, we conquer death.

Wondrous Bouquets of Glimmering Nature

In gardens lush, the blooms arise,
With colors bright, they mesmerize.
A tapestry of life unfolds,
In wondrous hues, a sight to hold.

The petals sway in gentle breeze,
As bees alight with playful ease.
Each blossom tells a tale of light,
Of summer days and starry night.

Through fields of gold and crimson red,
The whispers of the earth are spread.
A symphony of scents in air,
Awakens joy beyond compare.

With every fragrance, magic reigns,
In natural bouquets where love gains.
A treasure trove of memories,
In blooming hearts, the spirit frees.

Embrace the colors, let them guide,
Through wondrous paths where dreams collide.
In nature's hands, our souls will twine,
In glimmering grace, eternally shine.

Luminescence in the Lush Green Abyss

Amidst the foliage, shadows dance,
With flickers bright, they weave their chance.
The lush abyss, a vibrant scheme,
Awakens life, ignites a dream.

Each glimmer paints the night with lore,
In secret corners, myths explore.
The crickets sing in harmony,
Their voices blend with night's decree.

The leaves whisper secrets of the past,
While moonlight shimmers, spells are cast.
In every crevice, magic stirs,
Awakening the heart of hers.

The river glows with silvery threads,
As starlit echoes guide and spread.
Through emerald depths, where dreams collide,
In luminescence, we will abide.

So let us wander, lost in time,
Through verdant paths, where wonders rhyme.
In the lush green abyss, we find,
The light of life, forever kind.

Whispers of Twinkling Dew

In the hush of dawn's soft glow,
Glistening droplets dance so low,
Whispers of dreams the night must keep,
Awakening secrets from the deep.

Upon the blades of emerald grass,
Where shadows play and moments pass,
Nature's breath in tender sighs,
A world alive with waking eyes.

Beneath the branches, whispers sound,
The beauty of the night unbound,
Each pearl of dew a tale to share,
Of moonlit skies and wishes rare.

A tapestry of glimmering light,
Revealing wonders in the night,
With every drop, a story spun,
A dance of hearts where all begun.

In every whisper, magic speaks,
The essence of the earth that seeks,
To hold the dreams, the hopes, the dreams,
In glimmering dew, life gently beams.

Enchanted Spheres Beneath the Moon

Underneath the silver glow,
Enchanted spheres begin to flow,
Floating softly through the night,
Carried by the lunar light.

They twirl in dances, light as air,
Filling hearts with wondrous flair,
Casting shadows, weaving dreams,
In silent whispers, truth redeems.

Around the glow of ancient trees,
Their laughter mingles with the breeze,
Each sphere a story, lightbestowed,
A journey on a starry road.

In their presence, time stands still,
A potion brewed with gentle will,
Invoking magic from the past,
These spheres of light are seldom cast.

With every twinkle, secrets stir,
In the stillness, hearts confer,
Beneath the moon, in night's embrace,
Enchanted spheres, the world's grace.

Luminous Gems in the Mist

Amidst the fog, where shadows creep,
Luminous gems the secrets keep,
Shimmering softly, lost in day,
In gentle mists, they weave and play.

Each glimmer holds a tale untold,
A treasure of the brave and bold,
Reflecting dreams and fears alike,
Guiding hearts on paths to hike.

Twinkling softly, they serenade,
A whisper from the glen, a braid,
Of light and darkness, fate entwined,
Within the mist, solace defined.

As morning breaks, the gems will fade,
Yet in the memory, they stayed,
A dance of light in twilight's clutch,
In the heart, their spark ignites a touch.

In every breath of morning's air,
The gems of night still linger there,
A promise held in mist and dreams,
Luminous gems, bright as they seem.

Ethereal Globes in Mossy Embrace

In the forest's quiet grace,
Ethereal globes in mossy place,
Cocooned in soft, green velvet beds,
Where the whispering nature treads.

Glistening softly, light they share,
A magic spun with tender care,
They hold the dreams of seasons past,
In their embrace, the shadows cast.

With every pulse, a heartbeat sings,
In harmony with ancient things,
Wrapped in time, they sway so free,
A symphony of memory.

The morning dew on velvet moss,
Reflects the light of gain and loss,
As tender moments drift away,
The globes of dreams forever stay.

In twilight's glow, they flicker bright,
Guardians of the fading light,
Ethereal globes, forever known,
In their embrace, we are never alone.

Dreamy Glimmers by the Night Stream

In the hush of fading light,
Stars reflect on water bright,
Whispers dance in silver beams,
Flowing soft like fleeting dreams.

Moonlit trails on waves abide,
Glimmers spark where shadows glide,
Crickets sing in sweet refrain,
Echoing the night's domain.

Frogs croak low in soft duet,
Nature's song, a soothing net,
Glimmering orbs in robin's flight,
Guiding hearts through endless night.

Breezes wrap the world in grace,
Silken threads in twilight's lace,
Every ripple tells a tale,
In this realm where dreams set sail.

For beneath the ancient trees,
Mysteries unfurl like leaves,
Graceful sprites in shadows play,
Painting wonders in the sway.

Lush Orbs of the Arcane Wilds

In twilight woods where secrets lie,
Glowing orbs in emerald sigh,
Mushrooms dance with painted skin,
Whispers weave where spells begin.

Underneath the boughs, they glow,
Breathing life where few would go,
Flickering lights like fireflies,
Crafted from the earth and skies.

Ancient runes on bark unfold,
Stories waiting to be told,
Branches hum with magic's breath,
Life and dreams entwined with death.

Foxes prance through veils of mist,
While the spells of night persist,
Lush orbs pulse with secrets old,
In the wilds, they shape the bold.

Nature's canvas, wild and free,
Whispers dance like melodies,
In the heart of night they gleam,
Guarding every hidden dream.

Distant Pulses of Fairy Magic

In the distance, magic hums,
Where the heart of twilight drums,
Fairy lights like echoes bloom,
Chasing shadows through the gloom.

Tendrils weave in silver glint,
Painting paths of soft enchant,
Secret paths where few would tread,
Glimmers whisper tales unsaid.

With each pulse, the night awakes,
Beneath the branches, silence breaks,
Fluttering wings in shadowed flight,
Piercing through the veil of night.

From far away, sweet laughter springs,
Tales of joy that the starlight brings,
Distant pulses, weaving fate,
In the circle, love and hate.

In the dark where dreams expand,
Magic drifts like grains of sand,
Storytellers 'neath the stars,
Crafting wonders, healing scars.

Shaded Orbs Kissed by Twilight

In the fold of evening's sigh,
Twilight paints the weary sky,
Shaded orbs in cool embrace,
Magic lingers in this space.

Petals drop from gentle grace,
Kissed by twilight, time a trace,
Softly echoes of the day,
Whispers murmur, fade away.

Crickets play their twilight tunes,
Underneath the watchful moons,
Silvered lights adorn the glade,
In the warmth where dreams are made.

Fading shades of dusk unfold,
Magic secrets, stories old,
Foliage drapes in shadows deep,
Where the ancient spirits sleep.

So hush now, let the stars align,
In the twilight's glow, we'll find,
Shaded orbs softly arise,
Kissed by magic in the skies.

Woodland Treasures in Moonlight's Embrace

In the hush of the night, shadows play,
Whispers of leaves in soft ballet.
Moonbeams dance on the silver stream,
The forest glows with a dreamy gleam.

Mossy carpets, emerald and bright,
Glistening gems, a breathtaking sight.
Branches cradle the stars above,
Nature's gift, a promise of love.

A gentle breeze, a sweet perfume,
Ferns and flowers in twilight bloom.
The rustle of creatures, soft and shy,
As owls call their secrets to the sky.

Beneath the canopy, hearts entwine,
With echoes of magic in every line.
Dreams wander through this tranquil space,
Woodland treasures found in moonlight's grace.

Every shadow holds a story told,
Ancient wisdom in the night unfolds.
In this haven, time seems to cease,
A sanctuary of wild and wondrous peace.

Celestial Glow in Twilit Mist

As twilight drapes the world in glow,
A palette of colors begins to show.
Stars awaken, one by one,
A night of magic has begun.

The mist rolls in, a shroud of dreams,
Floating softly like whispered themes.
Moonlight spills on the silver dew,
Painting the night in shades anew.

Echoes of laughter from far-off places,
Filling the air with cherished traces.
Beneath the boughs, where secrets dwell,
A spell is cast, weaving a tale to tell.

Night's embrace, gentle and warm,
Promises shelter, a protective charm.
Under the sky, with hearts aglow,
In the celestial dance, we ebb and flow.

Each breath laden with starlit grace,
Time stands still in this sacred space.
The mysteries wrap us, closely intertwined,
In the glow of twilight, our souls aligned.

Esoteric Beads of Green Essence

Amongst the roots, a tapestry grows,
Whispers of nature in every pose.
Each bead of dew glistens and shines,
Treasures of earth within the pines.

Soft tendrils of ivy, delicate lace,
Embrace the trunks in a loving embrace.
Moss-covered stones keep secrets so dear,
Guardians of wonders, year after year.

A symphony hums through the whispering trees,
Invisible echoes carried by the breeze.
Leaves flutter softly, a soft serenade,
Nature's canvas, vividly displayed.

With every step, a story unfolds,
The essence of life in vibrant holds.
In shades of green, peace enchants the heart,
A mystical journey, a work of art.

Crickets choir as shadows appear,
The night unveils what we hold near.
In the forest deep, we find our way,
Through esoteric paths where spirits play.

Enigmatic Lights of the Fae Realm

In twilight's grasp, the colors swirl,
As flickering lights begin to unfurl.
The fae awaken, with laughter sweet,
Dancing lightly on silken feet.

Glowing orbs float on gentle streams,
Whispered secrets sprout as dreams.
A world beyond where time stands still,
In shadows cast, the heart must thrill.

Beneath the boughs, a shimmering shade,
A dance of magic in twilight played.
Wings like gossamer, soft and bright,
Weaving through the fabric of night.

With every flicker, a question stirs,
What mysteries lie where the magic blurs?
Wonders hidden just out of sight,
In the fae's realm, all is alight.

So follow the glow, let your spirit soar,
Through enchanted woods that ask for more.
In the embrace of the fae's charm,
The world comes alive, our hearts disarm.

Sylvan Echoes of Enchantment

In shadows deep where secrets dwell,
The ancient trees weave tales to tell.
Their whispers soft, a melodic breeze,
In twilight's grasp, the heart finds ease.

Beneath the boughs, the fairies play,
With laughter bright, they weave the day.
A shimmering dance on emerald glade,
In nature's arms, no fears invade.

Moonlit paths with silver sheen,
Guide wandering souls through realms unseen.
Each step a note in a timeless song,
Where every heart begins to belong.

Mossy carpets, soft and fair,
Cushion dreams beneath the air.
Flickering lights, the fireflies bring,
Magic wrapped in a silk-like string.

So linger here, let worries drift,
In sylvan corners, find your gift.
For in these woods, enchantments bloom,
And every heart can find its room.

Beheld by Woodlands and Starlit Dreams

In the canopy of deepening night,
Stars weave tales with a radiant light.
Woodlands pulse with a sighing breeze,
Where dreams unfurl beneath the trees.

Whispers float on the moon's soft rays,
Dancing shadows in a twilight haze.
Nature holds its breath, enthralled,
As nocturnal secrets are softly called.

A tapestry spun of ancient lore,
By starlit skies that forever soar.
The trees, like guardians, keep watch and keep,
While the world around them begins to sleep.

Echoes of magic drift through the air,
Dreams shared softly, secrets laid bare.
In twilight's embrace, all fears depart,
As the woodland cradles the yearning heart.

In this haven where shadows gleam,
Close your eyes and dare to dream.
For in the dark, the light still gleams,
Beheld by woodlands and starlit dreams.

Jewels of the Whispering Thicket

Amongst the thicket, hidden and shy,
Jewels of nature catch every eye.
Dewdrops glisten like stars on the ground,
In the quiet, simple beauty found.

Deep emerald leaves, they softly sway,
Guardians of secrets that dare not stray.
A melody weaves through the cool, crisp air,
Whispers exchanged with the world laid bare.

Sunlight dances on petals bright,
Illuminating paths in radiant light.
Each step uncovers a treasure rare,
Lullabies sung in the softest air.

From thorns to blooms, a journey unfolds,
In the heart of the thicket, magic behold.
With every rustle, a story's told,
In the whispers of leaves, the brave and bold.

So venture forth, let your spirit roam,
For in the thicket, you'll find a home.
With jewels of wonder, your heart will ignite,
As nature unveils her mystical light.

Glimmering Spheres Amidst the Ferns

In a twilight realm where shadows blend,
Glimmering spheres of light transcend.
Amidst the ferns, they softly glow,
A dance of dreams in the dusk's soft flow.

Illuminated whispers rise in the air,
Echoing stories of those who care.
Each sphere a keeper of hopes and fears,
Lighting the path through laughter and tears.

Beneath the starlit canopy's embrace,
Magic lingers in this sacred space.
Each twinkle a promise, each shimmer a song,
Binding the heart where it truly belongs.

Tenderly, the ferns cradle their light,
Guardians of dreams in the shroud of night.
In every flicker, a wish takes flight,
Glimmering spheres twinkling bright.

So wander here under the celestial dome,
In the wild, find your heart's true home.
For in the festival of light, you'll see,
The beauty of life, forever free.

Mirrored Drops in the Celestial Woods

In woods where whispers gently roam,
Mirrored drops like stars at home.
They catch the light of moons above,
Reflecting secrets, tales of love.

Beneath each leaf, a world awaits,
With mysteries that time creates.
Shimmering paths, both bright and dim,
Guide the heart on whims of whim.

Like glistening tears on emerald blades,
A dance of shadows softly fades.
Each ripple tells a tale untold,
Of magic's touch in green and gold.

Awakened dreams in twilight's grace,
Where nature wears her finest lace.
In mirrored drops, we find our way,
To secrets hidden, lost in sway.

Ethereal Pools of Enchanted Light

In quiet glades where soft winds sigh,
Ethereal pools reflect the sky.
Their shimmering depths, a calming sight,
Invite the soul to take its flight.

Beneath the surface, wonders dwell,
With whispers of a timeless spell.
Each glint revealing stories spun,
Of ancient magic, journeys begun.

In twilight's arms, the waters gleam,
As if they cradle every dream.
A gentle glow, a soft embrace,
These pools of light, a sacred place.

Ripples dance under moonlit beams,
Unfolding layers of whispered dreams.
In every drop, a universe,
Of hope and magic, free to traverse.

Celestial Glitter in Autumn's Grasp

As autumn winds begin to blow,
Celestial glitter starts to show.
Sparkling leaves, like flames in flight,
Adorn the woods with colors bright.

In every corner, beauty stays,
In fleeting moments, warm sunrays.
A golden canvas, nature's art,
Each shimmer a song, a budding heart.

The trees embrace the chilly air,
While whispers coax the leaves to share.
A tapestry of red and gold,
Where gentle stories of time unfold.

While dusk descends and shadows creep,
The glitter glows, its magic deep.
In autumn's grasp, there lies a spark,
A dance of light in the fading dark.

Resplendent Bubbles in a Dreamy Vale

In a vale where dreams take flight,
Resplendent bubbles catch the light.
They rise on breezes soft and sweet,
Carrying wishes, love's heartbeat.

Each bubble glimmers, floating high,
Reflecting whispers of the sky.
A fleeting world, so bright, so fair,
With laughter echoing through the air.

They bounce and play with gentle grace,
In this enchanted, timeless space.
With every pop, a joy unleashed,
As magic flows, and dreams are feasted.

In twilight's glow, the bubbles dance,
Creating memories, a wishful trance.
In this vale, our thoughts entwine,
Resplendent bubbles, dreams divine.

Phosphorescent Echoes in Fairy Tides

In whispered woods where shadows dance,
Beneath the moon's soft, silver glance,
The echoes of the fairies ring,
In tides of light, their voices sing.

With sparkling trails on water's skin,
They weave a world where dreams begin,
And every ripple tells a tale,
Of secret paths where magic prevails.

Each twinkling star, a guardian bright,
Guides wandering souls through the night,
While willow branches sway and bend,
To cradle dreams and joys transcend.

In twilight's grasp, the lanterns glow,
Illuminating hearts we know,
And in the silence, shadows play,
With phosphorescent grace, they sway.

So dance the tides of faerie lore,
On shimmering shores forevermore,
Where echoes linger, soft and sweet,
And magic and reality meet.

Etheric Glows in Eldritch Realms

In realms where time and space entwine,
The ether glows with threads divine,
A tapestry of night unfurled,
Hidden wonders wait, uncurled.

The ancient trees with whispers old,
Speak secrets of the brave and bold,
In gnarled roots, life's stories dwell,
Of echoes lost and tales to tell.

In shadows deep, where lost dreams fade,
The light of hope will not evade,
It bubbles forth in hues unknown,
To fill the hearts with warmth, its throne.

With every breath, the cosmos sighs,
A symphony of endless skies,
Each note a star, in harmony,
In eldritch realms where spirits flee.

So wander forth through veils of night,
Embrace the glow, let hearts take flight,
For in the depths of silence, glide,
In ether's glow, the magic bides.

Twilight Orbs and Celestial Dreams

As twilight paints the world in blue,
The orbs of light begin to strew,
A canvas rich with dreams untold,
Where wishes weave in threads of gold.

With every heartbeat, shadows blend,
In realms where night and stars descend,
The whispers of the cosmos flow,
To cradle hopes in quiet glow.

In silver streams where visions gleam,
The night unfolds its gentle theme,
And every sigh, a promise made,
In twilight's arms, fears start to fade.

So venture forth on paths of light,
Where dreams converge in soft twilight,
With every step, the cosmos sings,
Of hidden realms and secret kings.

In celestial realms where spirits soar,
Explore the wonders at your door,
For in each orb, a world awakes,
In twilight's clutch, the heart it takes.

Entranced by Nature's Subtle Magic

In morning dew where daisies gleam,
Nature whispers, stirs the dream,
The rustling leaves and songs of birds,
A symphony, without words.

With every breeze, a tale is spun,
Of ancient woods and shining sun,
And in the hush, the heart can feel,
The subtle magic, pure and real.

The petals bloom, a vivid shade,
A fleeting dance, a soft parade,
While shadows play on vibrant ground,
In nature's arms, our souls are found.

So tread the paths where wildflowers grow,
Let tranquil thoughts in silence flow,
For in the weave of every tree,
Awaits the magic, wild and free.

In gentle nights where starlight beams,
We find our hearts in nature's dreams,
Entranced by wonders all around,
In every whisper, magic found.

Fabled Spheres on a Decomposed Path

In the twilight's gentle sigh,
Fabled spheres begin to glow,
They whisper secrets of the sky,
As leaves of time begin to flow.

Beneath the boughs of ancient trees,
Hushed tales of yore softly weave,
Like beckoning fans in a spring breeze,
Inviting the wanderer to believe.

Each sphere a world, a distant lore,
Adorned with dreams of ages past,
Cradling echoes of the shore,
Where shadows and light hold steadfast.

Through tangled roots and winding trails,
We seek the fables they impart,
With every step, the silence wails,
Revealing the maps that dwell in heart.

An enchanted path, where whispers roam,
Carved by time, a painter's hand,
The fabled spheres guide us home,
Lighting our way through this strange land.

Sylvan Wonders in Shadowed Terrain

In shadowed terrain, where secrets keep,
Sylvan wonders softly gleam,
Under the watch of the willows deep,
A tapestry stitched from reader's dream.

Mossy stones tell tales of old,
Of fae and folk that danced at night,
Their laughter and mirth, a joy to behold,
In the moon's gentle, silver light.

Amidst the ferns, a rustle bright,
A flutter of wings, a hint of grace,
Where magic unfolds in the quiet night,
Embracing the stillness, a warm embrace.

The trees conspire, their branches sway,
To cradle the whispers lost in the breeze,
Sylvan wonders lead hearts astray,
Where dreams are painted with ease.

Beneath the stars, this sacred ground,
A garden of hope, a starlit flight,
In the shadowed terrain, we are bound,
To the wonders that shimmer in the night.

Celestial Bubbles in the Fern Grove

In the fern grove's soft embrace,
Celestial bubbles drift and sway,
Each a moment, a fleeting grace,
Caught in the dance of bright decay.

Like droplets of dew on leaves aligned,
They shimmer with colors rare and bright,
With every breath, the air intertwined,
Revealing worlds in ephemeral light.

Glimmering orbs, so tenderly spun,
Reflecting the dreams of those who roam,
In their depths, the stories run,
Of wandering souls far from home.

In this grove, where whispers soar,
The bubbles rise and softly fade,
Carrying wishes, and hearts that explore,
In their fragile forms, magic is made.

Nestled among roots and shaded glades,
Each bubble a promise, a shimmering thread,
In the fern grove's quilt where silence pervades,
A celestial dance of the dreamers led.

Veiled Jewels of the Whispering Woods

In the whispering woods, where shadows stream,
Veiled jewels glimmer amidst the dark,
Each a whisper, each a dream,
Sparkling softly, a hidden mark.

Woven through branches, where secrets lie,
They beckon the curious and wise,
In every breeze, a soft, sweet sigh,
Unraveling truths in nature's guise.

Glimmers of hope in the twilight's glow,
Embraced by the night, they softly gleam,
Illuminating paths that gently flow,
In the silence, they weave a dream.

As shadows dance and the moon takes flight,
These jewels whisper tales of the night,
Of wanderers lost, of love's delight,
Inducing the heart to take flight.

In the depths of the woods, a treasure untold,
Veiled jewels whisper beneath the sky,
Their stories, a tapestry, woven bold,
Awaiting the brave who dare to pry.

Shimmering Fantasies of the Enchanted Forest

In a glade where shadows dance,
The sunlight twinkles, takes its chance.
Mushrooms glow like stars at night,
Whispers travel, spirits in flight.

Canopy woven, twinkling bright,
Dreams are spun in soft moonlight.
Magic lingers in misty air,
Every step leads to a snare.

Wandering paths of emerald hue,
Creatures stir, both old and new.
Ferns unfurl with gentle grace,
The forest holds a secret place.

Echoes laugh from ancient trees,
Carried softly by the breeze.
Wishes blossom like morning dew,
In this world where dreams come true.

With every rustle, a story's told,
Of brave hearts and treasures bold.
The Enchanted Forest calls at dawn,
A realm where magic lingers on.

Elysian Orbs of the Sylvan Dream

Underneath the twilight's sigh,
Orbs of light begin to fly.
Each a tale of hopes and fears,
Floating softly, drying tears.

Crickets sing a lullaby,
As the moon begins to rise.
Stars above, like dreams they gleam,
In the heart of the sylvan dream.

Whispers weave through tender night,
Nature's pulse, a gentle might.
Every leaf holds magic's glow,
In the woods where secrets grow.

Cascading streams hum sweet refrains,
Reflecting worlds beyond the plains.
A sanctuary where hearts blend,
Lost in time, where dreams transcend.

Elysian orbs, so warm and bright,
Guide the wanderers of the night.
In every corner, hope is sown,
In this realm, we're never alone.

Tranquil Gems Amidst Whispering Leaves

Beneath the boughs, a hush prevails,
Softly singing, nature's tales.
Raindrops glisten on emerald glade,
Treasures of the world, unmade.

Gentle breezes share a tune,
Beneath the watchful silver moon.
Butterflies flit, colors ablaze,
Dancing through the twilight haze.

Lichen carpets the ancient stone,
Where time itself feels like a throne.
Crimson berries wear nature's crown,
In the quiet, calm renown.

Magic glows within each breath,
Life and dreams entwined with death.
A soft rustle, a sigh released,
Where tranquil gems, our souls are eased.

Whispering leaves reveal the past,
Echoes of love that ever last.
In this place, we cease to roam,
Amongst the whispers, we are home.

Radiant Secrets of Elfin Delights

In twilight's glow, the faeries sigh,
As starlight dances in the sky.
Glimmerings of laughter, sweet,
In hidden nooks, where shadows meet.

Elfin charms, with velvet grace,
Entwine the night in soft embrace.
With every twinkling, joy ignites,
In the heart of wondrous sights.

Petal-soft, their whispers weave,
A tapestry that none believe.
Magic drifts on gossamer wings,
In elfin lands, where freedom sings.

Candles flicker against the dark,
Each flame igniting nature's spark.
Amidst the glories of the night,
Radiant secrets whisper bright.

Elvin laughter trails behind,
Enigmas waiting to unwind.
Within the mist, enchantments kept,
Where hearts entranced, in wonder, slept.

Magical Orbs of the Hidden Vale

In the vale where shadows creep,
Orbs of light begin to leap,
Luminous whispers in the air,
Secrets of the night laid bare.

Colors dance on velvet mist,
Each a tale, an ancient twist,
Guiding souls who dare to roam,
Finding their way back to home.

With a shimmer, they collide,
Mysterious paths where dreams reside,
Embers of hope, bright and bold,
Stories lost, now retold.

Amidst the trees, they flicker bright,
Painting stars across the night,
In their glow, enchantments swell,
The magic of the vale to tell.

Through the silence, echoes sigh,
Underneath the vast night sky,
Orbs of wonder, soft and fair,
Inviting all to linger there.

Ethereal Lanterns Beneath the Evergreens

Beneath the boughs of ancient green,
Lanterns glow with secrets unseen,
Flickering softly, a guiding hand,
Leading souls through enchanted land.

In whispers low, they hum and sing,
Awakening dreams on gentle wing,
Filling the night with stories old,
Memories woven in threads of gold.

As twilight falls, they start to gleam,
Lighting pathways like a dream,
Shimmering softly, a tender sight,
Holding the magic of the night.

Their glow reflects in eyes so clear,
Each lantern a wish, a hope, a cheer,
Under the stars, they twinkle bright,
Guardians of the tranquil night.

Through the evergreens, spirits glide,
With each lantern, love and pride,
In this haven, hearts align,
Beneath the magic, souls entwine.

Twilight Wonders in Verdant Enclaves

In verdant enclaves, twilight falls,
A tapestry of shadowed calls,
Whispers of magic in the breeze,
Dancing softly through the trees.

Petals flutter, kissed by night,
Glimmers weave in soft twilight,
Each wonder lies in quiet grace,
Unveiling secrets of this place.

Softly glowed by moon's embrace,
Every corner holds a trace,
Of laughter, joy, and timeless lore,
In twilight's arms, we seek for more.

Reflecting dreams in pools of dew,
Every moment feels anew,
In this realm, we find our peace,
A gentle sigh, a sweet release.

The night unfolds its velvet shroud,
In whispers low, we stand unbowed,
For in these wonders, we shall find,
The heart of twilight, intertwined.

Enigmatic Lights on Humid Paths

Along the paths where silence reigns,
Enigmatic lights weave through the lanes,
A soft glow in the humid air,
Leading wanderers, unaware.

With a shimmer, they beckon near,
Casting doubts aside, no fear,
Memories flicker, alive and bright,
In the dance of the lingering light.

Each footstep echoes through the dark,
Guided by those sparks that spark,
Moments stolen, dreams take flight,
Illuminated by the night.

In twisting paths, they twist and glide,
A mystery wrapped in night's soft tide,
With every flicker, secrets glow,
The enchantment in shadows bestow.

Beneath the stars, we chase the trace,
Of enigmatic lights, a warm embrace,
In humid whispers, magic's hand,
Woven gently in this land.

Spheres of Enchantment in the Greenwood

In the depths of the ancient wood,
Whispers dance like a winding brook.
Moonbeams tease the hidden glade,
Where secrets in shadows softly look.

Each flower blooms with a knowing sigh,
Painting tales with colors bright.
The air is thick with magic's breath,
As day surrenders to the night.

Creatures small with glimmering eyes,
Converse with the winds in a gentle sway.
Stars descend like scattered dreams,
In the realms where enchantments play.

A gentle rustle, a fleeting breeze,
Brings forth the laughter of sprites unseen.
In twilight's embrace, they weave and spin,
A tapestry of the in-between.

Beneath the arch of the silvered boughs,
The heart of the forest sings anew.
In spheres of enchantment, time stands still,
Inviting the wanderer to pursue.

The Radiance of Fey and Fern

Amongst the ferns, where shadows play,
The fey emerge at break of day.
Their laughter light as the morning dew,
In a world where dreams and wonders brew.

Glimmers of gold in the sunlit air,
Whirl with the leaves in a dance so rare.
Each step they take, the earth does sigh,
As petals unfold to the cerulean sky.

With gossamer wings that catch the light,
The fey flit to songs of the night.
Through the tangled vines and the sparkling streams,
They guide the lost through the maze of dreams.

Every whisper carries a tale of yore,
Of ancient bonds and forgotten lore.
In their presence, the air feels alive,
Where the spirit of nature does thrive.

Beneath the boughs where shadows wend,
The radiance of fey invites to mend.
In the heart of the grove, enchantments swell,
A realm of magic, where all is well.

Ethereal Twilight in the Folkwood

As twilight descends with a silken brush,
The folkwood stirs in a gentle hush.
Stars blink awake in a dusky sweep,
While the world of dreams begins to creep.

Mossy carpets cradle every step,
While secrets in the night quietly prep.
The air is thick with sweet perfume,
As magic weaves through the twilight gloom.

A calling echoes from far and near,
Drawing forth the brave and the sincere.
With lanterns aglow, they travel in packs,
Into the heart, where joy never lacks.

Each leaf a witness, each branch a guide,
To stories whispered and love untied.
In this place where shadows bloom,
Ethereal twilight dispels the gloom.

With every flicker, a promise shared,
In the folkwood's heart, no soul is spared.
Where twilight wraps each dream in lace,
Awakening magic in an endless space.

Murmurs of Light upon the Leafy Veil

Beneath the leafy veil, where whispers dwell,
Murmurs of light begin to swell.
Each petal holds a spark divine,
In the shades of green, sweet dreams entwine.

Glimmers pulse like a heartbeat low,
Guiding wanderers where they ought to go.
Soft sonnets float on the breeze so light,
As the forest ignites with soft twilight.

Every branch a cradle for starlit sighs,
With echoes of magic that never die.
The night unfolds in a soft embrace,
Inviting all to find their place.

From roots that weave beneath the earth,
To the treetops singing of rebirth.
A symphony of shadows and beams,
Where every soul can share their dreams.

In the luster of night, through the leafy shield,
The murmurs of light in the forest revealed,
Embrace the moment, let worries fly,
In the haven of nature, where spirits sigh.

Mystic Spheres of Nature's Breath

In shadows cast by emerald trees,
Whispers dance upon the breeze.
Life awakens, soft and bright,
Beneath the moon's enchanting light.

From the brook, a song does flow,
Tales of ages long ago.
Mysterious orbs in twilight glow,
Guide the lost with gentle flow.

The stars in harmony align,
Each heartbeat tells of fate divine.
Nature's secrets softly weave,
In stillness, we dare to believe.

An echo in the mountain's heart,
Each note a piece, each sound a part.
The forest whispers, deep and true,
In every shade, a world anew.

Drawn to shores of ancient lore,
Where time stands still, forevermore.
In mystic spheres, the magic's cast,
A moment cherished, a spell that lasts.

Enchanted Candles in the Woodland Realm

In glades where moonlit wonders play,
The candles flicker night and day.
Each flame a guide, a watchful eye,
In the heart of woods where secrets lie.

With gentle hands, the fairies dance,
Around the light, they weave their trance.
Soft whispers wrap around the night,
Inviting dreams, both wild and bright.

The pine trees sway, in rhythmic tune,
Beneath the gaze of the silver moon.
In every glimmer, magic swells,
Enchanted stories, the silence tells.

Each candle burns, a spark divine,
Illuminating paths where spirits twine.
The air is thick with tales unfurled,
Of brave new worlds and wonders swirled.

As night descends in silver hue,
Hope dances lightly, bold and true.
In woodland realms, where hearts ignite,
Enchanted candles guide the night.

Glowing Spheres of the Dusk Enchantment

In twilight's grasp, the spheres emerge,
With colors bright, they softly surge.
A dance of light, a haunting call,
In dusky air, enthralling all.

The shadows stretch, a velvet cloak,
Each orb a promise, whispers spoke.
In gentle glows, the memories twine,
Of laughter shared, of dreams divine.

As dusk encroaches, mysteries bloom,
A sylvan path within the gloom.
The glowing spheres, like stars on earth,
Awaken dreams, rekindle mirth.

To every wanderer, a guiding flame,
A whispered hope, in night's sweet name.
The magic lingers, grows and flows,
In dusky realms, where wonder grows.

So step with care through evening's breath,
Where glowing paths defy the death.
Each sphere a spark of ancient lore,
Leading souls to evermore.

Veiled Radiance in the Thicket Dreams

In thickets deep where shadows play,
Veils of radiance drift and sway.
A hush surrounds the whispered night,
As dreams unfurl their silken flight.

With every breath, enchantments swirl,
A tapestry where fates can twirl.
In darkened corners, secrets bloom,
In veiled embraces, dispelling gloom.

Stars peek through the canopy high,
Glimmers catching the wandering eye.
In every rustle, magic sings,
In thicket dreams, where wonder clings.

A path unwinds with silvery grace,
Leading me to a hidden space.
Where veiled radiance ignites the mind,
And echoes of the past unwind.

So linger here where dreams are spun,
In thicket realms where shadows run.
Veiled radiance, a gentle stream,
Awakens hearts to the magic dream.

Dreamy Plumes of Verdant Charm

In twilight's glow, green whispers sigh,
Mossy blankets where secrets lie.
A breeze carries tales from high above,
Lulled by the chorus of the wood's soft love.

Beneath the boughs, where shadows dance,
Nature weaves its fleeting chance.
With every step, my heart takes flight,
Lost in the dreams of this gentle night.

Emerald spores with wishes contained,
In dreams, the mystic power reigned.
Floating softly on moonlit streams,
Here, every step feels like a dream.

Awake in the realm where silence sings,
Magic spins from unseen strings.
Lush plumes of hope rise all around,
In this enchanted world, love is found.

Opalescent hues dance on the glade,
Where fleeting moments are lovingly made.
These gifs of green, woven through air,
Whisper sweet thrills of a world so rare.

Gossamer Lights Through Enchanted Leaves

Gossamer threads in twilight's embrace,
Weave through branches, a delicate lace.
Stars twinkle softly, a guiding light,
Leading the wanderers through the night.

Leaves shimmer gently, kissed by the day,
With each breath, the shadows sway.
Dreamers gather, where whispers blend,
In this temple where magic won't end.

Golden glimmers find their home,
Amongst the fables of twilight's dome.
Stories flutter on fragile wings,
In the hush of evening, the heartstrings sing.

Time drips slowly, a shimmering stream,
Lighting the path through each tiny beam.
The world awakens, with sparkles aglow,
In the tangle of secrets that softly flow.

Starlit tendrils wrap the trees tight,
Inviting the dreamers to linger in light.
Through the leaves, a soft magic twirls,
As night envelops the dreaming world.

Glowing Vesicles of Fey Origin

Glowing orbs in twilight's embrace,
Dance and shimmer in secret space.
With every flicker, a story unfolds,
Of ancient enchantments, of legends retold.

They hover softly on breezy heights,
Carrying magic through the starry nights.
From realms beyond, their essence sings,
Of the hidden worth that dreaming brings.

In the cool of dusk, they pulse and glow,
Eager to guide those who wish to know.
They whisper softly in languages pure,
Inviting the brave, promising adventure.

Each step you take, they glimmer and sway,
Leading the seekers, lighting the way.
With laughter woven through their light,
They beckon you deeper into the night.

In their presence, worries fade away,
Vesicles of dreams where wishes play.
Through glades and groves, they hope to remain,
A beacon of wonder in the gentle rain.

Radiant Pearls in the Woodland Mist

Amidst the mist where secrets wait,
Radiant pearls and fate contemplate.
Shrouded in whispers of soft-spoken song,
The heart of the forest, where we belong.

Glistening dew on ancient bark,
Illuminates paths where the wild things hark.
Each pearl a promise, glimmering bright,
In the embrace of the velvety night.

Hushed tones echo through emerald halls,
Wrapped in the magic that twilight calls.
Time slows down as the world grows still,
Grazing the edges of dreams at will.

With every step, new wonders arise,
Crafted by starlight, spun from the skies.
These radiant treasures, hidden in mist,
Whisper of futures in moments unkissed.

In the hush of the dawn, their glow shall fade,
Yet the heart will remember the paths we've made.
Each luminous bead, a memory spun,
In this enchanted world, we're never undone.

Fae Lights Hanging on Mossy Ribbons

In twilight's embrace, they twinkle bright,
Fae lights dance softly, a wondrous sight.
They sway on ribbons, mossy and green,
Whispers of magic, where shadows convene.

Moonbeams shimmer on delicate rays,
Leading the lost through the night's soft haze.
With laughter and secrets, they guide the way,
Inviting the dreamers to join in their play.

A flicker of hope in the darkening glade,
These lanterns of nature weave spells unafraid.
They beckon the wanderers, hearts open wide,
In the hush of the forest, where magic resides.

Enchantments alive in the cool evening air,
Fae lights illuminate paths beyond compare.
Every glimmer a promise of realms yet unknown,
Within this cherished haven, no soul feels alone.

As dawn whispers secrets, the last glimmers fade,
But memories linger, forever displayed.
In the heart of the woods, where enchantments ignite,
Fae lights remain, luminous in the night.

Iridescent Pearls of the Stillness

In the quiet belly of the mossy brook,
Iridescent pearls lie, hidden from look.
They shimmer and dance in the gentle flow,
Guardians of stories the soft waters know.

Wrapped in the secrets of ages gone by,
They catch every tear that the world dares to sigh.
An echo of laughter, a whisper of woe,
These pearls of stillness through long moments flow.

On twilight's breath, in a silken embrace,
They glimmer like stars in a calm, quiet space.
Each drop holds a memory, each sway a dream,
Reflecting the truth of the forest's soft gleam.

Cascading through branches, they weave in and out,
Like threads of a tapestry, soothing all doubt.
Iridescent pearls, in their luster so fine,
Speak of the beauty in nature's design.

In stillness, they linger, endlessly bound,
To the rhythm of life in this vast, vibrant ground.
With gentle caresses, they cradle the night,
Holding the wisdom of each fading light.

Dreamlike Orbs Beneath the Glimmering Canopy

Dreamlike orbs dangle, a celestial sight,
Beneath the vast heavens, cloaked in soft light.
They twinkle like wishes on fingertips raw,
Spinning the magic of dreams we once saw.

In the canopy's shelter, where shadows entwine,
These worlds of illusion and hope intertwine.
Each orb tells a tale, a moment divine,
In the hush of the evening, where sweet dreams align.

They flutter like butterflies, delicate, free,
Marking the essence of all that can be.
With each gentle breath, they shimmer and swirl,
Inviting the dreamers to enter their world.

Awash in the hues of a twilight soft glow,
Dreamlike orbs float, where the wild rivers flow.
A dance of enchantment, a lullaby's grace,
Calling all wanderers to wander this place.

With beauty unbroken, they sway in the night,
Whispering secrets in the silvery light.
Beneath this vast shimmer, where dreams freely soar,
In the heart of the forest, forever explore.

Chromatic Gleams in the Enchanted Grove

In the depths of the grove where the wildflowers sway,
Chromatic gleams bloom in the soft light of day.
They giggle and shimmer like laughter released,
Painting the air with their joyous feast.

With each gentle rustle of leaves high above,
They dance in the wind, as if kissed by love.
Vivid hues born from the heart of the earth,
Whispering tales of the magic of birth.

When sunlight cascades through the branches so thick,
Chromatic gleams form a spellbinding trick.
They catch every ray, transforming the night,
Into a canvas where dreams take their flight.

In laughter and light, they weave through the trees,
Birthing bright colors that flutter like bees.
Each gleam a reminder of joys we once knew,
Everlasting echoes of wonder anew.

As twilight descends and the cosmos expands,
The chromatic gleams hold the world's dreaming hands.
Creating a tapestry, vibrant and bright,
In the heart of the grove, where all feels just right.

Resplendent Spheres of the Night Breeze

In shadows rich, the moonlight glows,
Whispers dance where the cool wind blows.
Stars like lanterns flicker and wink,
Painting secrets on the twilight's brink.

Gliding softly on silver streams,
Night's embrace cradles our dreams.
Each breath a note in this symphony,
Lost in the realms of reverie.

Awake, the owls stretch their wings wide,
Guardians of mysteries that abide.
Through ancient trees, their echoes tread,
Guiding the way where few have fled.

Glimmers of magic, ever so bright,
Beckon souls in the heart of night.
In the hush where time sways slow,
Linger now, let your thoughts glow.

Together we'll roam, hand in hand,
On the path where stardust stands.
Resplendent spheres in the night sky,
Cradle our spirits as we fly.

Luminous Treasures of the Arcane Woods

In the heart of woods where shadows loom,
Lies a treasure that chases gloom.
Dancing fairies with laughter so true,
Illumine paths with their radiant hue.

Cascading streams of crystal dreams,
Underneath the moon's soft beams.
The ancient oaks in silence, stand,
Guardians of secrets in this land.

Whispers float on the gentle breeze,
Carrying tales from the timeless trees.
Beneath the canopy where starlight plays,
Magic unfurls in mysterious ways.

As twilight deepens, shadows weave,
Drapes of night that we believe.
With every rustle and every sigh,
Luminous treasures twinkle nigh.

In the waltz of dusk, enchantments blend,
Stories of old without end.
In the arcane woods, hold not your fears,
For wonder thrives throughout the years.

Spellbound Drops in the Twilight Field

In a field where silence reigns deep,
Awaits the magic of dreams to keep.
Spellbound drops on the petals lie,
Catching the glow of the evening sky.

Gentle dewdrops twinkle like stars,
Held in the grasp of nocturnal czars.
Whispers of jasmine in the air,
Wrap us in scents beyond compare.

Each blade of grass a story unfolds,
Of secrets untold and legends bold.
In twilight's embrace softly we tread,
Where echoes of magic are gently spread.

The lantern fireflies begin their dance,
Inviting hearts to take a chance.
With every flicker, hope takes flight,
Transforming the dark with flickers of light.

Under the watchful gaze of the moon,
The night sings its sweet, soothing tune.
In this field where enchantments flow,
Hold tight to the wonders you know.

Starlit Orbs upon Gossamer Veils

Upon the hills where shadows blend,
Gossamer veils softly descend.
Starlit orbs like jewels aglow,
Woven in night's tender flow.

In twilight's hush, the world stands still,
Wrapped in the calm, a gentle thrill.
Dreams entwined with the midnight air,
Whispers of love linger everywhere.

The velvet sky, a canvas vast,
Holds the memories of the past.
Each twinkle spins a tale so bright,
A tapestry of dreams in flight.

As we wander 'neath this cosmic dome,
Our hearts awaken, finding home.
With every breath, we trace the light,
In the dance of stars, pure delight.

Starlit orbs guide each yearning soul,
Upon gossamer veils, we feel whole.
In cosmic rhythms, dreamers sway,
Forever enchanted, night turns to day.

Secrets of the Glade's Iridescence

In the glade where shadows twine,
Whispers of magic softly shine.
Hidden beneath the ancient trees,
A tapestry spun by the breeze.

Moonbeams dance on emerald leaves,
Carrying tales the forest weaves.
Each glimmer holds a story bright,
Secrets kept in the velvet night.

Crimson blooms with glistening dew,
Guard the tales of old and new.
In silence, they share their charms,
With the creatures who seek their arms.

Through the thicket, a shimmer trails,
Leading us to forgotten tales.
A flicker of light, a fleeting glance,
Invites us all to join the dance.

Echoes linger of laughter's sound,
As nature spins her world around.
In this glade, where dreams take flight,
The secrets glow in pure delight.

Luminous Spheres in the Woodland's Heart

In the heart of the woodland deep,
Luminous spheres begin to leap.
They float like wishes through the night,
Guiding lost souls with their light.

Underneath the silvered sky,
Whispers of magic pass us by.
Each glowing orb tells tales once told,
Of ages past and memories bold.

Among the roots where shadows play,
They mark the path and gently sway.
Crickets sing as the night unfolds,
The warmth of wonder their light holds.

Through tangled vines and mossy hair,
These spheres ignite the midnight air.
A wondrous glow for all to share,
Casting spells of joy everywhere.

As dawn approaches, they take flight,
Fading softly with the night.
In dreams, they linger, soft and fair,
Imprints of magic everywhere.

Veils of Mist and Glimmering Light

Veils of mist weave through the trees,
Softly caressing the whispering leaves.
In this sacred space, wonder blooms,
Where the sun breaks through morning's glooms.

Dewdrops twinkle like stars on grass,
Caught in the stillness as moments pass.
The air is thick with secrets untold,
Wrapped in wonders both soft and bold.

Glimmering light plays hide and seek,
In the soft silence, the forest speaks.
Each shimmer a promise, each blink a sigh,
Connecting the earth to the vast sky.

Along the brook where the fairies sigh,
Nature's chorus sings a lullaby.
Threads of light in the morning mist,
Breathe life into dreams that persist.

As day unfolds, the veils will part,
Revealing enchantments that fill the heart.
In every shadow and every light,
The magic of the woods ignites.

The Dance of Dew upon Gossamer Threads

In the dawn's embrace, dew drops gleam,
Dancing on threads like a fleeting dream.
Gossamer strands, delicate and fine,
Hold the whispers of the morning's shine.

A ballet of light upon the grass,
Each droplet's sparkle, a moment to pass.
As the sun kisses the world awake,
Nature's symphony begins to break.

With every sway of a gentle breeze,
The dance enchants the waking trees.
The forest stirs, alive with delight,
As droplets shimmer in the soft light.

Under canopies where shadows play,
Life awakens in a vibrant display.
The dew's quick step on a spider's weave,
Tells tales of wonder for those who believe.

This dance of nature, a sight so rare,
Reminds us all to stop and stare.
For in each drop, a world to hold,
A fragment of beauty, warm and bold.

Secrets of the Twilight Glades

In twilight's hush, the shadows creep,
Where secrets hidden gently sleep.
Whispers dance on the breeze so light,
In the heart of the glades, wrapped in night.

Moonbeams spill through leaves of gray,
Unraveling tales of a bygone day.
Echoes flutter in the dark,
Toward the dreams that leave their mark.

Each creature's song a cryptic code,
In the pathways where few have strode.
Magic entwines with every breath,
Guarded closely, as if from death.

Among the ferns, where fairies glide,
Lost in the glimmers of dreams they hide.
Time stands still, a fleeting sigh,
In the twilight glades where shadows lie.

So wander softly, with heart in hand,
For mysteries whisper across this land.
In twilight's embrace, find joy and fright,
In the secrets of the whispering night.

Mystical Beads of the Night

Each bead of night, a story spun,
From a time when magic had just begun.
They twinkle bright like stars in dreams,
Holding within, the moon's soft beams.

Woven within the fabric of fate,
A tapestry rich, no dream too late.
Each drop of dew, a soft delight,
Glistening sweet in the cool moonlight.

The night sings low, a haunting tune,
Carried by starlight, beneath the moon.
Wisps of wonder drift through the air,
In the presence of magic, nothing compares.

So gather the beads, those gems of night,
For within their glow resides pure light.
Mysteries deep, treasures to find,
In the dance of shadows, let dreams unwind.

A storybook world, alive with glee,
Where magical beads wait for thee.
In the shroud of darkness, they shall ignite,
The enchantment contained in the mystical night.

Glimmering Orbs in the Forest's Heart

In the forest's heart, where silence reigns,
Glimmering orbs dance, breaking chains.
With a flicker of light, they weave and spin,
In a world where enchantment shall begin.

Around ancient trees, faeries glide,
With laughter that stretches far and wide.
Each orb holds secrets, dreams untold,
A luminous treasure, a sight to behold.

As twilight descends, the magic thrives,
In the pulse of the forest, where wonder survives.
Soft murmurs echo through branches tall,
Calling to wanderers, enchanting all.

The glow softens fears, ignites the night,
Guiding the weary toward dream's light.
In every flicker, a promise waits,
In each gentle orb, destiny creates.

Closed eyes shall see, with heart so free,
The glimmering orbs, wild and carefree.
In the heart of the forest, join the dance,
As magic unfolds with a sweet glance.

Shimmering Drops of Eldritch Light

Underneath the arch of the ancient trees,
Shimmering drops drift on the breeze.
Each droplet's glow, a tale unsung,
Where whispers of magic have forever clung.

They trickle gently upon the ground,
A soft symphony; a magical sound.
From shadows emerging, they rise and gleam,
Illuminating paths through the heart of a dream.

In the spangled night, where wonders play,
Eldritch light dances, guiding the way.
With each droplet glistening, a secret's kept,
In the depths of the forest, where enchantments leapt.

Through dewdrops formed by moonlit sighs,
The world awakens, laying bare the skies.
Follow their shimmer, let your heart take flight,
With shimmering drops of the eldritch light.

So heed their call, embrace the night,
For in each shimmering drop, lies a spark of light.
In this magical realm, so vivid, so bright,
Dance with the shadows, taste the delight.

Mystical Reflections in the Dewy Night

In twilight's hush, the whispers roam,
A silver thread, weaving through the gloam.
Each droplet glints, a world anew,
Holding secrets known to but a few.

The stars conspire, a dance with grace,
While shadows play, in this hidden space.
A gentle breeze, like a soft embrace,
Carries the tales of time and place.

Beneath the boughs, the magic stirs,
With every heartbeat, the silence purrs.
The moonlight bathes the earth so bright,
Transforming dreams into the night.

Elusive forms in gentle sway,
In this enchanted, secret bay.
Nature sings in hushed delight,
In mystical reflections of the night.

A beckoning call, a voice we find,
In every sigh of the night wind.
And in each gleam, a promise made,
Of wonders waiting in the shade.

Moonlit Echoes upon Verdant Whispers

Upon the leaves, a lullaby,
As moonbeams dance in the sultry sky.
Each blade of grass, with secrets draped,
In verdant whispers, softly shaped.

The nightingale calls, its voice so clear,
As echoing tales drift near and dear.
With every note, the shadows play,
In harmony with the dreams that sway.

A shimmered path, where magic wends,
Unfolding stories that never end.
The canopy hums, a sweet refrain,
Underneath the stars, both wild and tame.

In every corner, life takes flight,
Illuminated by the gentle light.
The world transformed, so rich, so vast,
Each moment cherished, forever cast.

So linger here, in night's embrace,
Where nature whispers in a sacred space.
With every breeze, and rustle, sigh,
Moonlit echoes will never die.

Secrets of Luminescence in Nature's Lap

In twilight's glow, a spark ignites,
Secrets buried in fragile sights.
With glistening dew upon the ground,
Nature's whispers, a treasure found.

The fireflies twinkle like scattered stars,
Illuminating dreams from afar.
Their dance reveals the night's soft grace,
Awakening wonders in each hidden space.

Under the arch of a midnight sky,
The world holds its breath, letting out a sigh.
For in this moment, time stands still,
Each heartbeat echoes with tranquil thrill.

A canvas painted in shadows and light,
Crafting secrets within the night.
In every rustle, every knee-deep sigh,
The whispers of magic will never die.

So seek the treasures that lie within,
For every dusk prompts a new begin.
In nature's lap, the heart will leap,
To secrets of luminescence, we softly creep.

Glimmering Horizons in a Fairy's Caress

In meadows lush where wildflowers sway,
A fairy's touch guides the end of day.
With glimmering horizons dressed in gold,
Tales of old in twilight are told.

Across the brook, the shadows beam,
In whispered dreams, the soft light gleams.
Every petal holds a story bright,
In the heart of the enchanted night.

A sprinkle of magic hangs in the air,
With every wish, a lingering prayer.
For in the calm of nature's breath,
Lies the promise of love and rest.

These borders blend of earth and sky,
Where hopes take wing and doubts pass by.
In every sigh, a spark ignites,
With glimmering horizons, a choir of lights.

So follow the path, where fairies tread,
As fantasy blooms and doubts are shed.
For in their caress, we find our peace,
In glimmering horizons, our hearts release.

Shimmering Droplets in Sylvan Shadows

In the quiet woods where whispers dwell,
Droplets shimmer like a secret spell.
Nature's tears, a soft, glimmering light,
Dancing on leaves in the veil of night.

Silvery trails on emerald ground,
Echoes of magic in silence found.
Each drop a story, each gleam a dream,
Twinkling softly in the moon's beam.

Through tangled roots and ancient trees,
The droplets sway with the gentle breeze.
They guide the lost with their luminous glow,
Awakening wonders the heart longs to know.

Amidst the shadows, a melody sings,
Of hidden realms and their timeless things.
They sparkle brightly, yet often fade,
As daylight breaks and the night is laid.

In this sylvan embrace, hope finds a way,
To shimmer and shine through the dawn of day.
For even as they vanish from sight,
Their magic remains in the heart's delight.

Ethereal Orbs Beneath the Moon's Veil

Beneath the moon's soft, silvery veil,
Ethereal orbs in the night prevail.
Floating gently on whispers of air,
Each one a wish, a forgotten prayer.

They twinkle and dance like stars set free,
In a quiet waltz, a celestial spree.
With every pulse, they illuminate space,
Carrying dreams from a timeless place.

In gardens of shadows and silver light,
They weave a tapestry, serene and bright.
Secrets encased in their luminescence,
A symphony sung in quiet essence.

What stories lie in their gentle glow?
Of lost wanderers and love's sorrow.
They beckon the timid, the brave, the wise,
To find the magic that within them lies.

As dawn approaches, and they drift away,
Leaving behind a soft, dreamy sway.
Yet the night still lingers, a haunting call,
For those who seek, they shall never fall.

The Garden of Luminous Secrets

In a garden where the wild things grow,
Luminous secrets in twilight's glow.
Petals whispering tales of the past,
In every shade, a memory cast.

Radiant blooms in the soft moonlight,
Guarding mysteries until the night.
They sway to the rhythm of nature's song,
In the gentle embrace where they belong.

The air is alive with a seraphic scent,
Of dreams spun together, of magic bent.
In twilight's breath, each shadow concealed,
A tapestry woven, the unknown revealed.

With every step, new wonders unfold,
Stories of bravery and hearts bold.
In their glow, the secrets are shared,
Of laughter, of longing, of love laid bare.

As dawn whispers softly, these treasures fade,
Yet in our hearts, the glow is not swayed.
For this garden's magic, forever stays,
In luminous echoes of timeless days.

Gnarled Gems in Twilight's Embrace

Deep in the woods, where shadows cling,
Gnarled gems sparkle in twilight's wing.
Twisted branches, a mystical frame,
Guard what rests in this ancient game.

Each gem a heart, each twist a tale,
Of journeys embarked, of dreams set sail.
A silence profound, yet full of song,
In the night where forgotten souls belong.

Through tangled pathways, the secrets drip,
Of time long past, a well-worn script.
With every glance, a flicker, a gleam,
Echoes of hope in a darkened dream.

Here where the earth and night entwine,
Gnarled branches cradle the divine.
Each whispered breeze, a lover's sigh,
In twilight's embrace, the stars reply.

As dawn breaks gently, the gems recede,
Yet their whispers linger, a soft creed.
For though the night may wane and fade,
The gnarled gems in our hearts are laid.

9 781805 648000